MATHEMAGIC

Raymond Blum
Illustrated by Jeff Sinclair

Sterling Publishing Co., Inc.   New York

DEDICATION

This book is dedicated to my wife Gerri and my daughter Katie, for all the magic that they bring into my life.

Library of Congress Cataloging-in-Publication Data

Blum, Raymond.
    Mathemagic / Raymond Blum ; illustrated by Jeff Sinclair.
        p.   cm.
    Includes index.
    Summary: Dozens of number tricks from easy to expert.
    ISBN 0-8069-8354-X (trade)
    1. Mathematical recreations—Juvenile literature.
    [1. Mathematical recreations.]   I. Sinclair, Jeff, ill.   II. Title.
    QA95.B52   1991
    793.7′4—dc20   91-22523
                                          CIP
                                          AC

10 9 8

First paperback edition published in 1992 by
Sterling Publishing Company, Inc.
387 Park Avenue South, New York, N.Y. 10016
© 1991 by Raymond Blum
Illustrations © 1991 by Jeff Sinclair
Distributed in Canada by Sterling Publishing
% Canadian Manda Group, P.O. Box 920, Station U
Toronto, Ontario, Canada M8Z 5P9
Distributed in Great Britain and Europe by Cassell PLC
Villiers House, 41/47 Strand, London WC2N 5JE, England
Distributed in Australia by Capricorn Link Ltd.
P.O. Box 665, Lane Cove, NSW 2066
Manufactured in the United States of America
All rights reserved

Sterling   ISBN 0-8069-8354-X   Trade
                0-8069-8355-8   Paper

CONTENTS

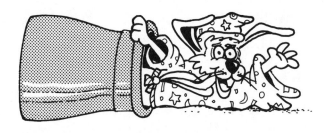

TO KIDS—BEFORE YOU BEGIN

You don't have to be a top student to perform these tricks, but after performing them for family and friends, you will look like a genius!

Here is what you need to know so that you will have the most fun with this book:

1. The tricks in each chapter are organized from the easiest to the hardest. Choose those tricks that are right for you.

2. Before you try working any trick, read the directions several times so that you thoroughly understand it.

3. Practice a trick by yourself first. When you have worked it through successfully two or three times, you are ready to perform it for your friends.

4. Don't worry if you make a mistake. You can always blame evil spirits for causing things to go wrong. Make up a magic spell that will drive them away, and then try the trick again or move on to a different trick.

5. Perform each trick slowly. If you take your time, you won't make careless errors and the trick will practically work itself.

6. Magicians never reveal their secrets. When someone asks you how a trick works, just say, "It's magic!"

7. Never repeat a trick for the same person. If people see a trick for the second time, they sometimes figure out how it's done.

Now you're ready to surprise and dazzle your family and friends. Good luck and, above all else, have fun!

INTRODUCTION—A NOTE TO PARENTS AND TEACHERS

Everyone loves magic! It's fun to watch and even more fun to perform for others. Here are dozens of number tricks for children of all abilities, ages nine and up. There are easy tricks for younger children and beginners, and there are more challenging tricks—including an "Extra For Experts" chapter for older children and teachers. With a little practice, children will be able to astound and entertain their family and friends or their entire class.

Number magic is easy to learn and perform because the tricks practically work themselves. There is no sleight of hand, and special magic skills are not required. No expensive magic equipment is needed and all supplies can easily be found in the home or purchased for minimal cost. Tricks have clear, uncomplicated, step-by-step instructions so that they are easy for children to read and understand.

Number magic adds variety and excitement to any math class and helps make learning fun. Teachers at any level will be able to perform these tricks for their students. All the tricks have been classroom tested and kids love them.

1. CALCULATOR CAPERS

BEWITCHED
GIVE ME 5!
TALKING CALCULATOR
SECRET CODE
FAMILY SECRETS
POCKET MONEY
HAUNTED CALCULATOR
SUBTRACTION SORCERY

BEWITCHED

Someone has placed an evil spell on your calculator. No matter which number your friend enters, it is ghoulishly transformed into the unlucky number 13!

Materials
A calculator

Presentation
Have a friend:

	Example
1. Enter in the calculator any number that is easy to remember —address, age, phone number, etc. (This number must be less than 8 digits.)	**77**
2. Double that number.	$77 \times 2 = 154$
3. Add 15 to that answer.	$154 + 15 = 169$
4. Triple that result.	$169 \times 3 = 507$
5. Add 33 to that total.	$507 + 33 = 540$
6. Divide that answer by 6.	$540 \div 6 = 90$
7. Subtract her original number.	$90 - 77 = 13$

This is a trick that can be repeated several times with the same friend. The final answer always ends up "unlucky"!

GIVE ME 5!

With your X-ray vision, you are able to see through the back of a calculator and reveal the number that appears in the display!

Materials

A calculator

Presentation

Have a friend:

	Example
1. Enter any number that is easy to remember in the calculator without letting you see it. (This number must be less than 8 digits.)	**365**
2. Multiply that number by 3.	**365 × 3 = 1,095**
3. Add 15 to that result.	**1,095 + 15 = 1,110**
4. Multiply that answer by 2.	**1,110 × 2 = 2,220**
5. Divide that result by 6.	**2,220 ÷ 6 = 370**
6. Subtract his original number from that total.	**370 − 365 = 5**

Finally, tell him to hold the *back* of the calculator towards you. Pretend that you have the power to see through solid objects, and then announce the total that appears in the display. No matter which number your friend chooses, the final total will always be 5!

Variations

When repeating this trick, change Step 3 and the final total will be a different number.

Step 3

Add	3	6	9	12	15	18	21	24	27	30→
Final Total	1	2	3	4	5	6	7	8	9	10→

TALKING CALCULATOR

Your friend secretly selects two numbers, works a few math problems, and hands you the calculator. When you hold the calculator up to your ear, it whispers the two numbers that she chose!

Materials

A calculator   Paper and pencil

Presentation

Have a friend write down a 1-digit number and a 2-digit number on a piece of paper without showing you.

Then hand her the calculator and ask her to:

	Example 6 & 82
1. Enter her 1-digit number.	**6**
2. Multiply that number by 5.	$6 \times 5 = 30$
3. Add 5 to that answer.	$30 + 5 = 35$
4. Multiply that result by 10.	$35 \times 10 = 350$

5. Add 20 to that total. $350 + 20 = 370$

6. Multiply that result by 2. $370 \times 2 = 740$

7. Subtract 8 from that answer. $740 - 8 = 732$

8. Add her 2-digit number to that result. $732 + 82 = 814$

Finally, ask her to hand you the calculator with the final total. Say that you are going to activate the calculator's talking mode by entering a special code. Subtract 132, push $=$, and your friend's two numbers will appear in the display.

$$\begin{array}{r} 814 \\ -\,132 \\ \hline \underline{6}\underline{82} \end{array}$$

Sneak a peek at the two numbers as you put the calculator up to your ear. Pretend that the calculator is whispering to you, and then announce your friend's two numbers!

An Exception
When you subtract 132 and get only two digits, your friend chose 0 for the 1-digit number.

Example	159
0 & 27	$-\,132$
	$27 = \underline{0}\underline{27}$

13

SECRET CODE

Your friend thinks of an important date in his life, and then works a few problems on a calculator. When he is finished, you enter a magical secret code and his date suddenly appears in the display!

Materials

A calculator   Paper and pencil

Preparation

Write this month chart on a piece of paper.

1-Jan.	4-April	7-July	10-Oct.
2-Feb.	5-May	8-Aug.	11-Nov.
3-March	6-June	9-Sept.	12-Dec.

Presentation

Ask a friend to think of any important date in his life—his birthday, for instance, or a favorite holiday.

Hand him the calculator and tell him to:

	Example
1. Enter the number of the month from the month chart without letting you see it. (September = 9)	**Sept. 10**
	9
2. Multiply that number by 5.	$9 \times 5 = 45$
3. Add 6 to that total.	$45 + 6 = 51$
4. Multiply that answer by 4.	$51 \times 4 = 204$
5. Add 9 to that total.	$204 + 9 = 213$
6. Multiply that answer by 5.	$213 \times 5 = 1,065$
7. Add the number of the day. (Sept. <u>10</u>)	$1,065 + 10 = 1,075$
8. Add 700 to that total.	$1,075 + 700 = 1,775$

Finally, tell your friend to hand you the calculator with the final total. Just enter the secret code (minus 865 equals) and the important date that he thought of will magically appear! The first digit is the number of the month, and the last two digits are the number of the day.

$$\begin{array}{r} 1775 \\ -\ \ 865 \\ \hline 910 \end{array}$$

↑ ↑
Sept. 10

An Exception

When you subtract 865 and get four digits, the first two digits are the number of the month.

Examples $1031 = \underline{10}\,\underline{31} = $ Oct. 31
$1205 = \underline{12}\,\underline{05} = $ Dec. 5

FAMILY SECRETS

After a friend works a few problems on a calculator, you are able to divulge how many brothers, sisters, and grandparents she has!

Materials
A calculator

Example
4 brothers
3 sisters
2 grandparents

Presentation
Have a friend:

1. Enter her number of brothers in the calculator.   **4**

2. Multiply that number by 2.   **4 × 2 = 8**

3. Add 3 to that total.   **8 + 3 = 11**

4. Multiply that answer by 5.	$11 \times 5 = 55$
5. Add her number of sisters to that total.	$55 + 3 = 58$
6. Multiply that answer by 10.	$58 \times 10 = 580$
7. Add her number of grandparents to that total.	$580 + 2 = 582$
8. Add 125 to that answer.	$582 + 125 = 707$

Finally, tell her to hand you the calculator with the final total. Just subtract 275 and her number of brothers, sisters, and grandparents magically appear!

$$\begin{array}{r} 707 \\ -275 \\ \hline 432 \end{array}$$

brothers → 4<u>3</u>2 ← grandparents

↑

sisters

Exceptions

When you subtract 275 and get only two digits, your friend has no brothers.

Example: 12 = <u>0</u>12 so number of brothers = 0.

When you subtract 275 and get only one digit, your friend has no brothers and no sisters.

Example: 2 = <u>00</u>2 so number of brothers = 0 and number of sisters = 0.

POCKET MONEY

After your friend works a few problems on a calculator, you are able to reveal his favorite number and how much loose change he has in his pocket!

Materials
A calculator

Presentation
Have a friend:

Example
Favorite Number-25
Loose Change-47¢

1. Enter his favorite number in the calculator. (This number must be five digits or less.) **25**

2. Multiply that number by 2. **$25 \times 2 = 50$**

3. Add 5 to that answer. **$50 + 5 = 55$**

4. Multiply that result by 50. **$55 \times 50 = 2750$**

5. Add the loose change in his pocket. (This amount must be less than $1.00) **$2750 + 47 = 2797$**

6. Multiply that total by 4. **$2797 \times 4 = 11188$**

7. Subtract 1000 from that answer. **$11188 - 1000 = 10188$**

Then, tell him to hand you the calculator with the final total. Just divide that total by 400 and your friend's favorite number and his loose change will magically appear!

$$10188 \div 400 = \underline{25}.\underline{47}$$

Favorite number

Loose change

Exceptions

If you divide by 400 and there is only one number after the decimal point, add on a 0 to get the loose change.

Example: $311040 \div 400 = 777.6 = \underline{777}.\underline{60}$
Loose change = 60¢

If you divide by 400 and there are no numbers after the decimal point, your friend has no loose change.

Example: $2800 \div 400 = 7. = \underline{7}.\underline{00}$
Loose change = 0¢

HAUNTED CALCULATOR

A supernatural power is summoned and asked for the year that your friend was born. Suddenly and mysteriously, the year appears in the calculator's display!

Materials

A calculator   Paper and pencil

Presentation
Have a friend:

1. Write down any 4-digit number on a piece of paper without letting you see it. Tell him that all four digits must be different.

2796

2. Rearrange the four digits in any order and write this new number below the first number.

9267

3. Subtract the two numbers on a calculator. Tell him to enter the larger number first.

$$\begin{array}{r} 9267 \\ -\ 2796 \\ \hline 6471 \end{array}$$

4. Add the digits of his answer together.
   If his answer has more than one digit, tell him to add those digits together until there is only one digit.

$6471 \rightarrow 6 + 4 + 7 + 1 = 18$

$18 \rightarrow 1 + 8 = 9$

5. Add 25 to that digit.

$9 + 25 = 34$

6. Add the last two digits of the year that he was born to that answer.

$34 + 80 = 114$

Finally, ask him to hand you the calculator with the final total. Say that you are going to ask the number spirits for assistance by entering a secret code in the calculator. Pretend to do some supernatural hocus pocus as you add 1866 to his total. When you push the equal sign, the year that he was born magically appears in the calculator's display!

$114 + 1866 = 1980!!!$

An Exception

For birthdays in the 2000's, add 1966.

SUBTRACTION SORCERY

You ask a friend to work a subtraction problem on a calculator. After she tells you just one digit of the answer, you are able to divulge the entire answer!

Materials

A calculator   Paper and pencil

Presentation   **Example**

Ask a friend to:

    1. Write any 3-digit number on a piece of
paper without letting you see it. Tell her
that all three digits must be different.   **427**

    2. Reverse this number and write it below
the first number.   **724**

    3. Subtract the two numbers on a   **724**
calculator. Tell her to enter the larger   **− 427**
number first.   **297**

Finally, ask her to tell you either the first digit or the last digit of the total. You are now able to divulge the entire answer!

How to Do It

Here are all the possible answers when you subtract two 3-digit numbers as described.

99 **198** **297** **396** **495** **594** **693** **792** **891**
(**099**)

Notice that the middle digit is always 9 and that the sum of the first digit and the last digit is 9. So just subtract what your friend tells you from 9 to get the missing digit.

Example

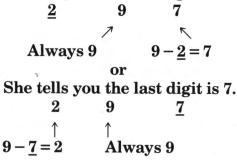

She tells you the first digit is 2.

<u>2</u>   **9**   **7**

Always 9   **9 − <u>2</u> = 7**

or

She tells you the last digit is 7.

2   **9**   <u>7</u>

9 − <u>7</u> = 2   **Always 9**

An Exception

If your friend tells you that the first digit or last digit is 9, her answer will be 99.

22

2. CARD CONJURING

SWITCHEROO
ELEVEN IN A ROW
CRYSTAL BALL
INVISIBLE DECK
ABRACADABRA
FOUR ACE BAFFLER
MYSTERIOUS FORCE
POCKET PUZZLER

SWITCHEROO

A deck of cards is divided into two piles. Your friend secretly takes a card from each pile and places it in the opposite pile. Even though each pile is thoroughly shuffled, you are able to find your friend's two cards!

Materials

A deck of playing cards without Jokers

Preparation

Put all the even cards in one pile (2, 4, 6, 8, 10, Queen) and all the odd cards in another pile (Ace, 3, 5, 7, 9, Jack, King). Shuffle each pile so that it is well mixed.

Presentation

1. Have your friend shuffle each pile separately without looking at the cards. Spread both piles face down on the table.

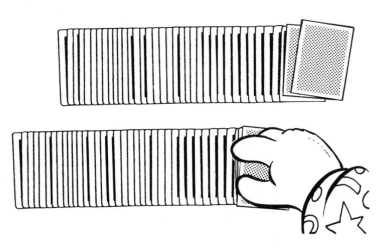

2. Tell her to choose one card from the group at the top, look at it, and place it in the group on the bottom. Then have her choose a different card from the group at the bottom, look at it, and place it in the group on the top.

3. Have her shuffle each pile, put one pile on top of the other, and hand you the deck of cards. Within seconds, you are able to reveal her two cards!

How to Do It

The odd card that is chosen will be surrounded by even cards, and the even card that is chosen will be surrounded by odd cards.

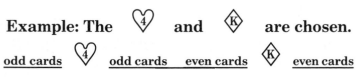

ELEVEN IN A ROW

Eleven cards are placed face down in a straight row on a table. After you leave the room, your friend moves some of the cards. When you return, you are able to tell how many cards were moved even though the row looks exactly the way it did when you left the room!

Materials
A deck of playing cards

Preparation
Take the following eleven cards out of the deck: Any Joker and any cards from Ace through 10. Place them face down on a table in order in a straight row.

J oker	A	2	3	4	5	6	7	8	9	10

Left   *(All cards should be face down)*   **Right**

Presentation

1. Tell your friend that when you leave the room, he should move some cards from the left end of the row to the right end of the row, *one card at a time*. He may move any number of cards from 0 to 10.

2. Before you leave the room, move some of the cards yourself to show him how they should be moved. You are really doing this to get your *Key #*.

Example
You move 3 cards.
(This is your *Key #*—remember it!)

Left **J oker** **A** **2** **3** **4** **5** **6** **7** **8** **9** **10** **J oker** **A** **2** Right

27

3. Leave the room and have your friend move some of the cards.

Example
He moves 5 cards.

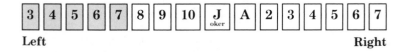

Left   Right

4. When you return, perform some hocus pocus and pretend that the cards are speaking to you. Tell your friend that the cards will reveal the number of cards that he moved. Remember your *Key #* and count over that many cards from the *right end* of the row. Turn this card over and the number on that card will tell you how many cards your friend moved! (The Joker = 0 and Ace = 1.)

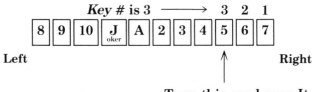

Turn this card over. It is a 5 so your friend moved 5 cards.

A Variation
Use a different *Key #* each time you perform the trick.

CRYSTAL BALL

Your calculator becomes your magical crystal ball when it mystically reveals a 2-digit number that is concealed inside a deck of cards!

Materials

A deck of playing cards   A calculator

Preparation

Remove all the 10s and face cards from a deck of cards so that your deck has only Aces through 9s.

Presentation

Ask your friend to shuffle the deck, remove two cards without looking at them, and place them face down on the table. The rest of the deck can be set aside.

Tell him to secretly look at either card and memorize its number (Ace = 1). Its suit is not important. You look at the other card, and then both cards are returned face down on the table. Put your card one inch to the right of your friend's card. Explain that the two cards represent a 2-digit number and that the calculator will be your crystal ball that will reveal that number.

Example
Friend's Card—9
Your Card—3

Hand your friend the calculator and have him:

1. Enter the number of his card.   9

2. Multiply that number by 2. $9 \times 2 = 18$

3. Add 2 to that result. $18 + 2 = 20$

4. Multiply that answer by 5. $20 \times 5 = 100$

5. Subtract the Magic Number.
*The Magic Number is
10 minus your card number.*
     $(10 - 3 = 7)$ $100 - 7 = 93$

Finally, have your friend turn over the two cards on the table. The 2-digit number that is formed by the two cards will match the number that appears in the crystal ball!

INVISIBLE DECK

After your friend picks a card from your "invisible deck" and works a few problems on a calculator, you are able to announce the name of her invisible card!

Materials

A calculator   Paper and pencil

Preparation

Write these charts on a piece of paper.

Card Numbers   **Value of Suits**

Ace = 1	Clubs = 1
2 = 2	Diamonds = 2
3 = 3	Hearts = 3
↓ ↓	Spades = 4
10 = 10	
Jack = 11	
Queen = 12	
King = 13	

Presentation

Pretend to have an invisible deck in your hands. Shuffle it thoroughly, and then ask a friend to pick a card from your "deck." Tell her to write the name of her card on a piece of paper.

Example: 7 of Hearts

Hand her the calculator and ask her to:

1. Enter the card's number.   **7**

2. Add the number that is one more than this number.
$(7 + 1 = 8)$ $7 + 8 = 15$

3. Multiply that result by 5. $15 \times 5 = 75$

4. Add the value of the suit to that answer. (Hearts = 3) $75 + 3 = 78$

5. Add 637 to that result. $78 + 637 = 715$

Then, tell your friend to hand you the calculator with the final total. Just subtract 642 and her card will magically appear!

$$\begin{array}{r} 715 \\ -642 \\ \hline 7\,3 \end{array}$$

7 of Hearts

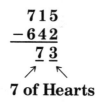

An Exception

When you subtract 642 and get three digits, the first two digits are the card's number.

Example: 124

Queen of Spades

A Variation

Perform the trick with two or more friends at the same time. Before you announce their cards, pretend to $+$, $-$, $\times$, and $\div$ their totals so that they will think that their answers are somehow related to each other.

ABRACADABRA

Your friend mentally chooses a card from a pile of 21 cards. When the magic word "ABRACADABRA" is spelled out, your friend's chosen card suddenly appears!

Materials
A deck of playing cards

Presentation
1. Shuffle the deck, count out 21 cards, and set the rest of the deck aside.

2. Deal out three piles of seven cards each, face down on the table. Deal the cards from left to right, one pile at a time, as if you were dealing to three players in a card game. There is no need for you ever to see the faces of any of the cards.

3. Ask your friend to choose one of the piles. Take the pile that he chose in your hand, fan out the cards to-

wards him, and ask him to mentally select any card.

4. Put the pile that he chose between the other two piles so that you again have a pack of 21 cards in your hand.

5. Once more, deal out three piles of seven cards each, face down on the table. Taking up one pile at a time, fan out the cards towards your friend and ask him which pile has his chosen card. Again, put the pile that has his chosen card between the other two piles so that you have a pack of 21 cards in your hand.

6. Repeat Step 5 one more time.

7. Tell your friend that you are going to say the magic word "ABRACADABRA" and his chosen card will magically appear. Slowly spell "ABRACADABRA," turning over one card for each letter. The last card that you turn over will be your friend's chosen card!!

FOUR ACE BAFFLER

Three cards are randomly removed from the deck and they are all Aces! Then the "number spirits" are summoned and the fourth Ace mysteriously appears!

Materials
A deck of playing cards

Preparation
Put an 8 card in the eighth position down from the top of the deck and put the four Aces in the ninth, tenth, eleventh and twelfth positions.

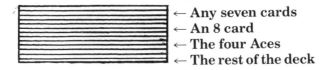
← **Any seven cards**
← **An 8 card**
← **The four Aces**
← **The rest of the deck**

Presentation

1. Ask a friend for a number *between* 10 and 20. (*Caution:* 10 will work, but 20 will not.)

Example
13

2. Deal that number of cards into a small pile one card at a time. Place the rest of the deck next to the small pile.

 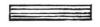
← **13 cards**

3. Ask your friend to add the digits of that number.

$13 \rightarrow 1 + 3 = 4$

4. Return that many cards to the top of the big pile one card at a time.

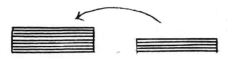
Return four cards

5. The top card of the small pile will be an Ace! Turn this card face up and show your friend.

6. Set the Ace aside and put the small pile on top of the big pile.

7. Repeat the six steps with two *different* numbers between 10 and 20 to remove two more Aces.

Finally, pretend to do some supernatural hocus pocus as you ask the "number spirits" for a sign to help you find the last Ace. Pretend that they tell you to turn over the top card. It will be an 8. Count down eight more cards and the eighth card will be the fourth Ace!

MYSTERIOUS FORCE

You secretly predict which card will be chosen from the deck, and then the "number spirits" mysteriously force your friend to choose that card!

Materials

A deck of playing cards, complete with 52 cards plus two Jokers

Paper and pencil
A calculator, if needed

Presentation

1. Have your friend shuffle the cards as many times as she wants.

2. When she hands you the cards, say that you forgot to take out the Jokers. Turn the cards over, remove the Jokers, and sneak a peek at the bottom card. This is the "predicted card."

3. Secretly write the name of the "predicted card" on a piece of paper, fold it several times, and put it aside until later.

4. Tell your friend that a supernatural mathematical power will force her to choose your predicted card.

5. Deal out twelve cards face down from the top of the deck and spread them out on the table. Ask your friend to turn any four of these cards face up.

6. Put the other eight cards on the *bottom* of the deck.

Example

7. Hand your friend the deck and tell her to deal cards face down below each of these cards. She should start with the number on the face up card (All face cards = 10 and Aces = 1), and then keep dealing cards until she gets to 10. For example, if the face-up card is a 6, she would deal four more cards to get to 10.

37

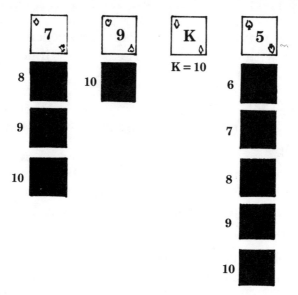

K = 10

8. Tell her to keep the four face up cards on the table and put all the face down cards on the *bottom* of the deck.

9. Ask her to find the sum of the four cards:

$$(10)$$
$$7 + 9 + K + 5 = 31$$

10. Have her count down that many cards in the deck and turn the last card face up. (Turn card #31 face up.) This is her chosen card. Finally, unfold your prediction and show your friend that it matches her chosen card!

A Variation

If your deck of cards has no Jokers, sneak a peak at the bottom card after your friend hands you the deck.

38

POCKET PUZZLER

Your friend removes four cards from the deck and secretly puts one of them in her pocket. After performing some number magic on a calculator, you are able to reveal the card that is hidden in your friend's pocket!

Materials

A deck of playing cards   A calculator
Paper and pencil

Presentation

1. Ask your friend to write any 4-digit number on a piece of paper without letting you see it. Tell her that all four digits must be different.

Example
8756

2. Tell her to add the four digits together and write the sum below the first number. $(8 + 7 + 5 + 6 = 26)$

−   26

3. Have her subtract the two numbers, using a calculator.

8730

4. Hand her the deck of cards and ask her to secretly remove four cards that have the same numbers as the four digits. (Ace = 1 and 0 = King) Also, tell her that each card must be of a different suit.

Example
8 = 8 of Hearts
7 = 7 of Clubs
3 = 3 of Diamonds
0 = King of Spades

5. Tell her to put one of the cards *that is not a King* in her pocket, and then hand you the other three cards.

Example: She puts the 3 of Diamonds in her pocket and hands you the 8 of Hearts, the 7 of Clubs, and the King of Spades.

6. Mentally add the values of these three cards.

$$8 + 7 + 0 = 15$$

If your answer has more than one digit, add the digits together until there is only one digit.

$$15 \rightarrow 1 + 5 = 6$$

7. Mentally subtract this number from 9, and the value of the card that is in your friend's pocket will magically appear.

$$9 - 6 = 3$$

The card that is in your friend's pocket is a 3 and since the only suit that is missing is Diamonds, your friend's card is:

The 3 of Diamonds!

An Exception

When you mentally subtract from 9 and get 0, your friend's card is a 9—not a King.

3. MEMORY MAGIC

WHAT'S ON YOUR MIND?
WHAT'S THE DIFFERENCE?
BRAIN WAVES
MISSING DIGIT
THE HUMAN CALCULATOR
MEMORY WIZARD
EXTRASENSORY PERCEPTION
MIND READING

WHAT'S ON YOUR MIND?

Your friend randomly selects a 2-digit number. You are able to read his mind and reveal the number that he is thinking of!

Materials

10 scraps of paper   A shoe box

Presentation

1. Ask your friend to name any 2-digit number.

2. Write that number on a scrap of paper, fold it several times, and drop it into a shoe box. Make sure that no one sees what you are writing.

3. Repeat Steps 1 and 2 several times until your friend has named about ten different numbers.

4. Have your friend reach into the shoe box and open up one of the scraps of paper without letting you see it.

5. Rip up the remaining scraps of paper so that their powerful mathematical vibrations will not interfere with your mindreading.

6. Ask your friend to concentrate on the number that he is holding. Pretend that you are reading his mind, and then reveal that number!

How to Do It

Write the first number that your friend names on *every* scrap of paper. If every scrap of paper has the same number, it will be very easy to tell him what's on his mind!

WHAT'S THE DIFFERENCE?

Your friend will be amazed when you correctly predict the answer to a subtraction problem. Then, when she works a different problem, you are able to read her mind and reveal that answer, too!

Materials

A calculator   Paper and pencil

Preparation

Secretly write a prediction (198) on a piece of paper, fold it several times, and put it aside until later.

Presentation

Example

1. Ask your friend to write down any three-digit number whose digits are in decreasing order.

765

2. Then tell her to reverse this number and write it below the first number.

− 567

3. Finally, have her subtract the two numbers on a calculator.

198

The answer will always be 198!

When your prediction is opened, it matches her answer!

4. Next, tell your friend to follow the same directions with any four-digit number whose digits are in decreasing order. Tell her not to show you the answer.

$$\begin{array}{r} 3210 \\ - \ 0123 \\ \hline 3087 \end{array}$$

The answer will always be 3087!

Ask your friend to concentrate on the entire answer. Pretend that you are reading her mind as you reveal that the answer is 3087!

A Variation

A humorous variation on the three-digit trick is to open your prediction upside down.

Your friend will think that you have made a mistake until you turn the answer over and it reads:

BRAIN WAVES

This is a trick that you and your friend can perform together. After you leave the room, your friend asks someone to choose a number. When you return, not a single word is spoken yet you are able to reveal the chosen number!

Materials
None

Preparation
Practice with your friend before performing the trick for others.

Presentation
1. You leave the room and your friend asks someone to choose any number from 1 to 10.

2. When you return, tell your friend to concentrate on the chosen number. By laying your hands on your friend's head, you are able to hear his thoughts and reveal the chosen number!

How to Do It
When you put your hands on your friend's head, place your fingertips on his temples. If your friend keeps his mouth closed and slightly tightens his jaw, you will be able to feel movement under your fingertips. So if the chosen number is seven, your friend tightens his jaw seven times. With a little practice, no one will be able to see your friend's jaw move and you should have no trouble receiving his "brain waves"!

MISSING DIGIT

Your friend works a subtraction problem and tells you all the digits of her answer except for one. Within seconds, you are able to reveal the missing digit!

Materials

A calculator   Paper and pencil

Presentation

1. Have your friend write down any 4-digit number without letting you see it.

Example
2759

2. Tell her to add the four digits together and write the sum below the first number. $(2 + 7 + 5 + 9 = 23)$

−   **23**

3. Ask her to subtract the two numbers.

2736

4. Tell her to circle any digit in her answer that is *not* 0.

2⑦36

5. Ask her to slowly read off the remaining digits in any order. After a few seconds, you are able to reveal the circled number!

How to Do It

Mentally add the digits that your friend reads to you.

$$2 + 3 + 6 = 11$$

If your answer has more than one digit, add those digits together until there is only one digit.

$$11 \rightarrow 1 + 1 = 2$$

Mentally subtract that number from 9 and the missing digit will magically appear!

$$9 - 2 = ⑦$$

An Exception

When you add the remaining digits together and end up with 9, your friend circled a 9.

Example:
$$\begin{array}{r} 8962 \\ - 25 \\ \hline 8⑨37 \end{array}$$ $8 + 3 + 7 = 18 \quad 18 \rightarrow 1 + 8 = ⑨$

A Variation

This trick will work for any number of digits. Ask your friend to choose the 8-digit serial number from any dollar bill.

THE HUMAN CALCULATOR

You can amaze your friends by adding five 3-digit numbers in just a few seconds!

Materials

Paper and pencil   A calculator

Presentation

1. Ask a friend to write a 3-digit number on a piece of paper. The digits must be different and may not form a pattern.

2. Ask him to write a second number below his first number.

3. Ask him to write one more number. This third number is your *Key #*. ──────────→

4. You write a three-digit number so that the sum of the first and the fourth numbers = 999.

5. You write a three-digit number so that the sum of the second and the fifth numbers = 999.

6. Give your friend the piece of paper and ask him to add the five numbers using the calculator without letting you see the Final Total.

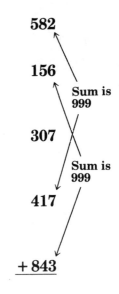

582

156

Sum is 999

307

Sum is 999

417

+ 843

(2,305)

When he returns the paper to you, pretend that you are adding the five numbers in your head, and then write down the Final Total in one or two seconds!

How to Do It

When your friend hands you the paper, all you have to do is look at the *Key #*, because the Final Total is:

$$2000 + (Key\ \#\ -\ 2)$$

Example: Key # is 307. $307 - 2 = 305$

The Final Total: 2,000
+ 305
2,305

An Exception

Your friend writes a 9 for the first digit of the first number or the second number.

50

Example

Sum is 999

$$\begin{array}{r} 824 \\ 961 \\ 602 \\ 175 \\ \underline{38} \end{array}$$

Sum is 999

← Write a 2-digit number. Don't put a zero in the first place.

Variations

Using seven three-digit numbers, follow the same procedure and the Final Total is:

3000
+(Key # − 3)

Using nine three-digit numbers, follow the same procedure and the Final Total is:

4000
+(Key # − 4)

MEMORY WIZARD

Your friends are amazed that you are able to memorize a 26-digit number!

Materials
Paper and pencil

Preparation
Write this on a piece of paper:

$$35,831,459,437,077,415,617,853,819$$

Put this on a second piece of paper:

——, ——, ——, ——, ——, ——, ——, ——, ——

Presentation
Hand your friend the piece of paper that has the 26-digit number written on it. Tell her that you have memorized the number and that you would like her to test you. Show her that there are no numbers written on the second piece of paper, and then write down all 26 digits!

How to Do It
You don't have to memorize the entire number. Just remember the first two digits, and then add to get the remaining 24 digits.

1. Write down the first two digits.   **35**

2. To get the next digit, mentally add those 2 digits together.

$$3 + 5 = \underline{8}$$ **35,$\underline{8}$**

3. Mentally add the last two digits to get the next one. If this sum is 10

or greater, write down only the
number that is in the ones place.

$$5 + 8 = 1\underline{3} \qquad\qquad 35,8\underline{3}$$

4. Continue adding the last two
digits to get the next one until you
have written down all 26 digits.

$8 + 3 = 1\underline{1}$	35,83\underline{1}
$3 + 1 = \underline{4}$	35,831,\underline{4}
$1 + 4 = \underline{5}$	35,831,4\underline{5}
$4 + 5 = \underline{9}$	35,831,45\underline{9}
$5 + 9 = 1\underline{4}$	35,831,459,\underline{4}

and so on until you get:

35,831,459,437,077,415,617,853,819!!

A Variation

Prepare a number that is longer than 26 digits and you
will really impress your friends!

15,617,853,819,099,875,279,651,673,033,695

EXTRASENSORY PERCEPTION

You prepare a deck of 30 index cards, each with a different number written on it. When the blank side of a card is shown to your friend, he is able to tell you whether the number on the other side is odd or even!

Materials

30 blank index cards   pencil

Preparation

Write a different number from 1 to 30 on each card.

Presentation

Have your friend sit across the table from you. Tell him that you have reason to believe that he has psychic powers and that you have developed a test to prove it. Shuffle the cards thoroughly and then put one even card and one odd card face up on the table.

Fan out the rest of the index cards in your hand. Be careful that your friend doesn't see any of the numbers. Then hold up one card at a time—*blank side* facing your friend—and ask him if the number on the other side is odd or even. (Pretend that you are choosing cards randomly from different parts of your hand but actually choose all 14 even numbers first!)

If your friend says "Even," put the card *face down* on the left pile. If he says odd, put the card *face down* on the right pile.

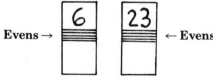

Evens →   **← Evens**

When all fourteen even cards are down, turn one even card over and put it face up on the right pile. Take one of the odd cards from your hand (they will all be odd) and put it face up on the left pile.

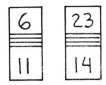

Hold up the remaining cards one at a time as before. This time, if your friend says odd, put the card face down on the left pile. If he says even, put the card face down on the right pile.

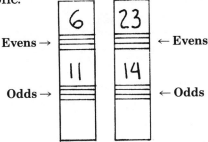

At this point, the left side is correct and the right side is incorrect. Gather up the cards on the left side and hand them to your friend so that he can see how well he did.

As he is looking at those cards, gather up the cards on the right side and secretly move the face-up odd card (23 in the example) to the top of the pile. This move will make the right side correct.

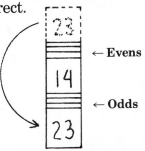

Finally, show your friend that the right side is correct too. He won't believe that he got them all right! He will think that he has E.S.P.!

A Variation
Use playing cards instead of index cards.

MIND READING

You can amaze your friends with your mindreading powers. Here, you reveal their deepest mathematical thoughts, and then you look into the future and predict which card will be chosen from the deck!

Materials
A deck of playing cards   Paper and pencil

Preparation

Put your favorite card at the bottom of the deck. Example: 10 of Hearts

Number a blank piece of paper from 1 to 3.

Presentation
1. Show your friend that there are no answers written on the piece of paper. Then tell her to think of any math

word—"Fraction," for example. Pretend that you are reading her mind and write your favorite card (10 of Hearts) *after #3* on the paper. Don't let your friend see what you are writing and she will think that you are writing her math word after #1. Ask her which math word she thought of. When she tells you, smile as you look at the paper and say, "Great."

2. Tell your friend to think of any 3-digit number (907, for example). Pretend that you are reading her mind and then write her math word (Fraction) *after #1* on the paper. Ask her which 3-digit number she thought of. When she tells you, repeat her 3-digit number and say, "Terrific."

3. Tell your friend that you are going to predict which card will be chosen from the deck. Pretend to be deep in thought as you write her 3-digit number (907) *after #2* on the paper.

```
1. Fraction
2. 907
3. 10 of ♡
```

4. Ask your friend to cut the deck into two equal piles. Tell her that you are going to count to see how well she did. Ask her to count the cards from the top half of the deck while you count the cards from the bottom half. If you count your pile one card at a time, your favorite card will come to the top. Take your pile and put it on top of her pile to complete the cut. Your favorite card is now at the top of the deck.

5. Finally, unfold the paper and show your friend that the math word and the three-digit number are correct. Read your prediction and then have her turn over the top card of the deck. It matches your prediction!

4. FUNNY STUFF

HOW TO BECOME AN INSTANT MILLIONAIRE

This is a trick that you can play on your mom or dad. It shows you how to turn a penny into millions of dollars!

Materials
2 sheets of paper   Pen

Preparation
Copy the "contract form" and the bill onto the two sheets of paper.

Presentation
Tell your parents that you are going to do the dishes every night for the next 30 days. (Trust me—please read on.) Say that they don't even have to give you your regular allowance anymore. Tell them that you only want 1¢ for doing the dishes the first night, 2¢ for the second night, 4¢ for the third night, double that to 8¢ for the fourth night, and so on. If they agree, have them sign a contract like the one shown here.

CONTRACT

I, _____, agree to pay _____
　　　Parent's Name　　　　　　　　　　Your Name
1¢ for doing the dishes the first night, 2¢ for the second night, 4¢ for the third night, double that to 8¢ for the fourth night, and so on for the next 30 days.

_____
Parent's Signature

After they sign this contract, present them with their bill. It will be quite a shock, so have them sit down first!

THE BILL

DAY	PAY
1	$.01
2	$.02
3	$.04
4	$.08
5	$.16
6	$.32
7	$.64
8	$1.28
9	$2.56
10	$5.12
11	$10.24
12	$20.48
13	$40.96
14	$81.92
15	$163.84
16	$327.68
17	$655.36
18	$1,310.72
19	$2,621.44
20	$5,242.88
21	$10,485.76
22	$20,971.52
23	$41,943.04
24	$83,886.08
25	$167,772.16
26	$335,544.32
27	$671,088.64
28	$1,342,177.28
29	$2,684,354.56
30	$5,368,709.12
GRAND TOTAL	**$10,737,418.23!!!**

MATH WITH MUSCLE

This number trick will show you how to do hundreds of situps in just a few seconds!

Materials

A watch or clock

Presentation

Tell your friends that you are going to do between "two and three hundred situps" in less than one minute. Be careful that you don't say, "between two hundred and three hundred situps"! Have a friend time you and when he says, "Go," just sit down and do five situps. After all, 5 is between 2 and 300!

IN$TANT CA$H

This is a great math joke that shows you how to turn a small investment into thousands of dollars of profit—magically—in just a few days!

Presentation

Tell your parents that you have a great idea for how they can invest their money. Explain that if they do exactly as you say, they will make over $8,000 in less than a week! (That should get their attention.)

Here's your financial advice:

First, they should build a medium-size animal pen in the backyard. Tell them that you will help and that it won't cost very much money.

Second, they should go to a local pig farmer and buy five female pigs (five sows). They should have them delivered to your backyard and put in the animal pen.

Finally, they should go to a wildlife farm and buy five male deer (five bucks). They should have them delivered to your home and put in the pen with the pigs.

That's it! If your parents have followed your financial advice, they now have five pigs and five deer in their backyard pen and they just made over $8,000!

Your parents will probably think that you've lost your mind! They won't understand—until you explain to them—that in just a few days they have turned a small investment into 10 sows and bucks (10 thousand bucks)!

HAND CALCULATOR

Your friends are amazed when you magically transform your hands into a calculator and multiply on your fingers!

Materials

Pen

Preparation

Draw these calculator keys on your palms with a ballpoint pen.

Presentation

Tell your friend that she can multiply *by 9* on your hands just as she would on a regular calculator. After she enters the numbers and pushes ⊟ , just bend over the finger that is multiplied by 9. The fingers that are standing up tell her the answer!

Example: 9 × 4 = 36

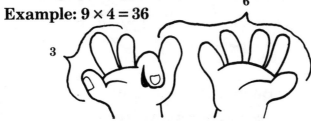

Bend over finger #4

Example: $9 \times 8 = 72$

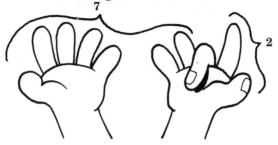

Bend over finger #8

An Exception

Example: $9 \times 10 = 90$

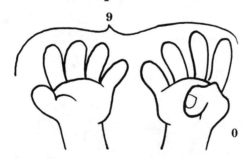

Bend over finger #10

<u>9</u> fingers on the left and <u>0</u> fingers
on the right = <u>9</u> <u>0</u>.

?!? THE 3½ OF CLUBS?!?

A card that is sealed in an envelope has exactly half the value of a randomly selected card. The trick works even if the selected card is odd!

Materials

A deck of playing cards
   with a Joker
A calculator
An envelope
Tape

Preparation

Photocopy the 3½ of Clubs on this page and then tape or laminate it over one of the Jokers.

Seal the 3½ of Clubs inside an envelope.

Put the 7 of Clubs in the fifth position down from the top of the deck.

Presentation

Tell your friend that he will randomly select a card from the deck and that the card in the envelope will have exactly half the value of his selected card.

Example: If he selects the 10 of Hearts, the 5 of Hearts will be in the envelope.

**Example
(555) 246-4468**

Hand your friend the calculator and have him:

1. Enter his phone number.	**2464468**
2. Multiply that number by 10.	**24644680**
3. Subtract his phone number from that answer.	**22180212**
4. Divide that total by his phone number.	**9**
5. Subtract the number of digits in his phone number (7 digits) from that answer.	**2**
6. Add the number of digits in his area code (3 digits) to that answer.	**5**

Announce once more that the card in the envelope will have exactly half the value of the randomly selected card. Ask your friend for his total (it will always be 5), count down that many cards in the deck, and turn over the fifth card—the 7 of Clubs.

Your friend will think that you have made a mistake, because an odd number can't be divided in half evenly. Will he be surprised when he opens the envelope!

½ of the 7 of Clubs is the 3½ of Clubs!

A Variation

There is a way of shuffling the cards so that the 7 of Clubs remains in the fifth position down from the top. Divide the deck into two piles and riffle the ends together allowing the two piles to interweave. Let the top seven to ten cards fall last and the 7 of Clubs will remain in the fifth position no matter how many times you shuffle. Practice this many times before you try it with a friend.

THE NAME OF THE CARD IS . . .

You secretly predict which card will be chosen. Then you ask a friend to randomly select a number and count down that many cards in the deck. At first this card doesn't match your prediction, but after a few comical adjustments, the name of the card mysteriously appears!

Materials

A deck of playing cards   A calculator
Paper and pencil

Preparation

Put the 10 of Hearts in the eighteenth position down from the top of the deck.

Presentation

Announce that you are going to predict which card will be chosen from the deck. On a piece of paper, write:

THE NAME
OF
THE CARD IS

Fold the paper so that your friend doesn't see what you've written and put it aside until later.

Ask your friend to:

	Example
1. Enter a 3-digit number into the calculator. (The first digit must be larger than the last digit.)	**845**
2. Reverse this number and subtract it from the first number.	**− 548**
	297

3. Add the digits in the answer.

$$2 + 9 + 7 = 18$$

The digits will always add up to 18!

Tell him to count down that many cards in the deck. It will be the *10 of Hearts*. Finally, ask him to open the piece of paper and read your prediction. He'll read, "THE NAME OF THE CARD IS". Say that you were in such a hurry that you forgot to finish your prediction. Then make these adjustments and his card will mysteriously appear!

—cross off the H in THE	T̶H̶E N̶A̶M̶E̶	TEN
—cross off the AME in NAME		
—cross off the T in THE	OF	OF
—cross off the CD in CARD		
—change the I in IS to a T by crossing the top	T̶HE C̶A̶R̶D̶TS	HEARTS

4½ CENTS

You tell your friend that the number of pennies hidden in your hand is exactly half the number that he will randomly choose. Hold it! What happens if he chooses an odd number?

Materials

5 pennies   A calculator
Paper and pencil

Preparation

You will need help to prepare for this trick. Have an adult bend a penny back and forth with two pairs of pliers until it breaks in half.

Hide 4½ pennies in your hand.

Presentation

Tell your friend that the number of pennies hidden in your hand is exactly half the number that he will choose at random.

1. Ask him to write down any number that has 8 digits or less. Tell him that all the digits must be different.

Example
19,573

2. Have him rearrange the digits in any order and write this new number below the first number.

93,175

3. Ask him to subtract the two numbers using a calculator. Tell him to enter the larger number first.

93,175
− 19,573
73,602

4. Tell him to add the digits of his answer together.

$$73,602 \rightarrow 7 + 3 + 6 + 0 + 2 = 18$$

If his answer has more than one digit, tell him to add those digits until there is only one digit.

$$18 \rightarrow 1 + 8 = 9$$

The final answer will always be 9!

Your friend will think that you have made a mistake because ½ of 9 is 4½. How can you have 4½¢? Open your hand and show him!

2 HALVES = 1 HOLE

You show your friend how to cut a large band of paper into 2 separate loops. This is very easy to do, but when your friend tries, she ends up with something entirely different!

Materials
A pair of scissors   A newspaper
Cellophane tape

Preparation
Cut out four-inch-wide strips of newspaper. Tape them together to make two seven-foot strips.

Take one of the seven-foot strips of paper and tape the ends together to make one large band.

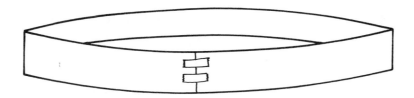

Do the same with the second seven-foot strip, but give one end of the strip a half twist before taping the ends together.

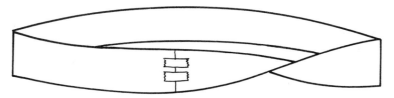

Presentation

Show your friend how easy it is to cut a band of paper into two separate loops. Use the band that does not have the half twist. Carefully cut straight down the middle until you get back to where you started and you will end up with two separate pieces.

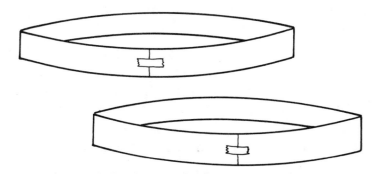

Give your friend the pair of scissors and the band with the half twist. She won't notice the half twist if you lay the band in a small pile on a table in front of her. Tell her to carefully cut straight down the middle until she ends up with two separate loops. It looked so easy when you did it, but she won't be as lucky. It's impossible to cut this band into two separate pieces. A band with a half twist actually has only one side, so it stays in one piece when cut in half. She'll end up with a giant 14-foot loop!

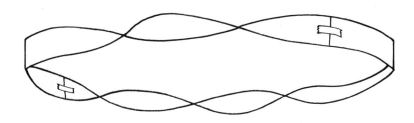

Variations

Here are some other tricks that you can try by yourself. Use shorter strips of paper that are about three inches by 28 inches.

1. Give one end of a strip of paper *two* half twists (1 full twist) before taping the ends together. Cut straight down the middle of the band until you get back to where you started. If you cut carefully, you will end up with 2 loops!

2. Give one end of a strip of paper a half twist before taping the ends together. Instead of cutting down the middle as before, cut one inch in from the right edge of the band. Keep cutting until you go around the band *twice* and get back to where you started. You will end up with two loops again, but the result will surprise you!

3. Experiment with more twists and different cuts and see what happens. What do you think would happen if you cut your friend's 14-foot loop straight down the middle? Try it and see!

??7 × 13 = 28??

Your friends are thoroughly confused when you "prove" to them that $7 \times 13 = 28$!

Materials

Paper and pencil

Presentation

Only a number magician could prove that $7 \times 13 = 28$. Here are three different ways to prove it. If you talk fast enough, you will be able to fool your friends.

FIRST WAY—MULTIPLICATION

7 times 3 equals 21 and
7 times 1 equals 7.
$$21 + 7 = 28$$

So: $7 \times 13 = 28$!!

$$
\begin{array}{r}
13 \\
\times\ 7 \\
\hline
21 \\
+\ 7 \\
\hline
28
\end{array}
$$

SECOND WAY—DIVISION

7 does not divide into 2, but it does divide into 8 one time. Put down the 1 and subtract 7. That leaves 21. 7 divides into 21 three times.

$$
\begin{array}{r}
13 \\
7\,\overline{)\,28} \\
7 \\
\hline
21 \\
\underline{21}
\end{array}
$$

You multiply to check division.

If $\quad 2\,\overline{)\,8}^{\,4} \quad$ then $\quad 2 \times 4 = 8$

So, if $\quad 7\,\overline{)\,28}^{\,13} \quad$ then $\quad 7 \times 13 = 28$!!

THIRD WAY—ADDITION

Multiplication is repeated addition so 7×13 is seven thirteens added together.

Add up the column of 3's and get 21. Then add down the column of 1's and get 7 more ($21 + 7 = 28$).

So: $7 \times 13 = 28$!!

$$
\begin{array}{rrr}
(22) & 13 & (21) \\
(23) & 13 & (18) \\
(24) & 13 & (15) \\
(25) & 13 & (12) \\
(26) & 13 & (\ 9) \\
(27) & 13 & (\ 6) \\
(28) & +13 & (\ 3) \\
\hline
& 28 &
\end{array}
$$

5. ODDS AND ENDS

HOCUS POCUS

MAGICAL LINKING PAPER CLIPS

SUM FUN

BELIEVE IT OR NOT

TIME WILL TELL

KNOT THAT FINGER

SECRET WORD

HOCUS POCUS

You ask your friend to choose any domino when your back is turned. When the magic words "Hocus Pocus" are entered in a calculator, the number of dots on each part of the domino suddenly appear!

Materials
A set of dominoes
A calculator

Presentation
You spread a set of dominoes out on a table, and then ask your friend to secretly choose one.

Example

Hand him the calculator and tell him to:

1. Enter one of the domino's numbers.
(Blank = 0)   **<u>3</u>**

2. Multiply that number by 5.   **3 × 5 = 15**

3. Add 7 to that answer.   **15 + 7 = 22**

4. Double that total.   **22 × 2 = 44**

5. Add the domino's other number to
that result.   **44 + <u>6</u> = 50**

Finally, tell your friend to hand you the calculator with his answer. Enter the magic words "Hocus Pocus" by pushing

As you push the buttons, say "Ho-Cus-Po-Cus," and the number of dots on both parts of the domino will magically appear!

$$50 - 14 = \underline{3}\,\underline{6}$$

(If your friend had entered the 6 first, your final total would have been $\underline{6}\underline{3}$.)

Exceptions

When your friend chooses a domino with one blank and enters the 0 first, your final total has only one digit.

Example: The final total is 5.
$5 = \underline{0}\,5$ so the domino has a blank and a 5.

When your friend chooses a domino with two blanks, your final total will be 0 because $0 = \underline{00}$.

MAGICAL LINKING
PAPER CLIPS

Two paper clips are magically joined together without anyone touching them. And, when a rubber band is added, all three become linked together by some mysterious mathematical force!

Materials

4 paper clips
A 3-inch (7.5 cm)
   rubber band

A strip of paper—
3 × 11 inches
(7.5cm × 27.5 cm)

Presentation

Curve a strip of paper into an S-shape. Then attach two paper clips so that it looks like this:

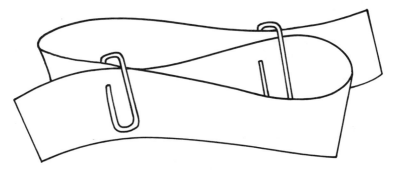

Slowly pull the ends of the paper apart in the direction of the arrows. When the two paper clips are almost touching, pull harder and they will magically join together!

Next, loop a rubber band around the strip of paper before attaching two more paper clips so that it looks like this:

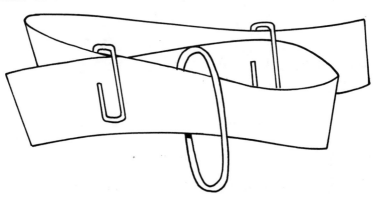

When you pull the ends of the strip of paper apart, the paper clips will be linked together and hanging from the rubber band, which is still attached to the strip of paper!

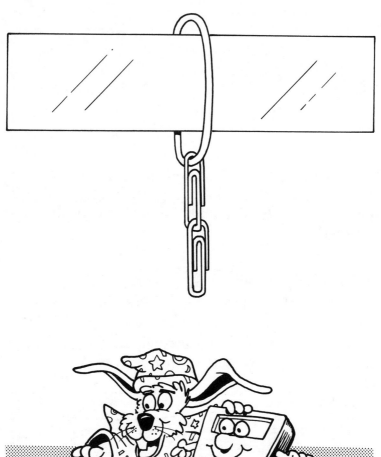

Variations

Attach two paper clips on each side of the strip of paper and you end up with four paper clips joined together. Try other variations and see what happens.

Instead of a strip of paper, use a dollar bill.

SUM FUN

Numbers are written on both sides of some index cards. When your back is turned, your friend mixes them up and turns some of them over. You are able to announce the sum of all the numbers that are showing without ever looking at them!

Materials

5 index cards or pieces
   of paper

A calculator

Preparation

Write a "1" on one side of an index card and a "2" on the other side. In the same way, write a "3" and "4" on a second index card, a "5" and "6" on a third, a "7" and "8" on a fourth, and a "9" and "10" on a fifth.

Presentation

Hand your friend the five index cards. Tell her to mix them up, turn some over, and lay them out on the table when your back is turned.

Example

Have her find the sum of the five numbers using a calculator.

$$1 + 8 + 4 + 5 + 10 = 28$$

Ask her how many of those numbers are odd (1, 3, 5, 7, 9).

"There are two odd numbers."

Mentally subtract this number from the "Magic Total," which is 30, and you will get the sum of all 5 numbers!

$$30 - 2 = 28$$

| **Magic Total** | **two odd numbers** | **The Sum** |

Variations

Change the number of index cards and subtract from a different Magic Total.

Index cards	Numbers	Magic Total
6	11 & 12	42
7	13 & 14	56
8	15 & 16	72
9	17 & 18	90
10	19 & 20	110

BELIEVE IT OR NOT

When your back is turned, your friend chooses a magazine at random and concentrates on one of the pages.
Unbelievably, you are able to read his mind and describe
what appears on that page!

Materials
10 magazines or books   A calculator

Preparation
Put 10 magazines in a row on the table.
Study page 27 in the fourth magazine.

Presentation
Hand your friend the calculator and have him:

	Example:
1. Enter any number between 1 and 100.	**50**
2. Add 28.	$50 + 28 = 78$
3. Multiply by 6.	$78 \times 6 = 468$
4. Subtract 3.	$468 - 3 = 465$
5. Divide by 3.	$465 \div 3 = 155$
6. Subtract 3 more than his original number $(50 + 3 = 53)$.	$155 - 53 = 102$
7. Add 8.	$102 + 8 = 110$
8. Subtract 1 less than his original number $(50 - 1 = 49)$.	$110 - 49 = 61$
9. Multiply by 7.	$61 \times 7 = 427$

The final total will always be 427!

With your back turned, tell your friend to look at the first digit of his final total, count over that many magazines, and remove it from the row. Then tell him to look at the last two digits of his final total and turn to that page number in the magazine.

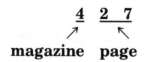

Finally, ask him to concentrate on that page for about 30 seconds. You should have no problem "reading his mind" and describing what appears on that page, since you studied it before the trick started!

TIME WILL TELL

Your friend mentally selects any hour on the face of a clock. After performing some number magic, the clock reveals the hour that he is thinking of!

Materials

A clock or a picture of
a clock drawn on
a piece of paper

A pencil

Presentation

Ask your friend to think of any hour on the clock without telling you. Explain that you are going to point randomly to different numbers on the clock while he silently counts up to 20. Tell him to start with the hour that he is thinking of and add one every time you point to a number.

> **Example: He's thinking of 8:00 so he counts
> 9 when you point to the first number,
> 10 when you point to the second number,
> etc.**

When he gets to 20, he should say, "Stop!", and your pencil will be pointing to the hour that he is thinking of!

How to Do It

As your friend is counting up to 20, you are counting, too. The first seven numbers that you point to can be any numbers on the clock. However, the eighth number must be 12. Then go backwards around the clock until your friend tells you to stop.

Example: Your friend is thinking of 8:00.

He counts:	9	10	11	12	13	14	15	16	17	18	19	20 Stop!
You count:	1	2	3	4	5	6	7	8	9	10	11	12
You point to:	any number							12	11	10	9	8:00

KNOT THAT FINGER

This is a trick that you can do for a group of your friends or relatives. While you are out of the room, a string is tied around someone's finger and everyone hides their hands. When you return, you work some number magic and within seconds, you can tell who has the string! You are also able to reveal the hand and the finger that the string is tied on!

Materials

A calculator   Paper and pencil
A piece of string

Presentation

Pick one of your friends to be your assistant, and then number the rest of your friends starting with #1. While you leave the room or turn your back, have your assistant tie a string on someone's finger. Also, tell her to write down that person's number and the hand and finger that has the string. Tell everyone to hide their hands.

Example
Friend #7
Left Hand Fourth Finger

Hand your assistant the calculator and have her:

1. Enter the number of the
person who has the string.   **7**

2. Multiply that number by 2. $7 \times 2 = 14$

3. Add 3 to that result. $14 + 3 = 17$

4. Multiply that answer by 5. $17 \times 5 = 85$

5. Add 8 if the string is on the
right hand.
   Add 9 if the string is on the
left hand. $85 + 9 = 94$

6. Multiply that total by 10. $94 \times 10 = 940$

7. Subtract 46 from that result. $940 - 46 = 894$

8. Add the number of the finger
(The thumb is 1.). $894 + 4 = 898$

9. Add 600 to that total. $898 + 600 = 1498$

Finally, ask your assistant to hand you the calculator with the final total. Just subtract 774 and you will be able to find that string!

$$
\begin{array}{r}
1498 \\
- \ 774 \\
\hline
724
\end{array}
$$

Number → 724 ← Number
of   ↑   of
Person   Hand   Finger
        1 = right
        2 = left

An Exception

When you subtract 774 and get four digits, the first two digits are the number of the person.

$$
\begin{array}{r}
\textbf{Example:} \quad 2687 \\
- \ 774 \\
\hline
1913
\end{array}
$$

Person #19 → 1913 ← Third Finger
                ↑
          Right Hand

SECRET WORD

A friend looks through a book and secretly selects a word on any page. After performing some number magic, you are able to find her selected word from the thousands of words in the book!

Materials

A book with at least   A calculator
  100 pages   Paper and pencil

Presentation

Ask your friend to turn to any page in
the book and write down its page   **Example**
number without letting you see it.   **Page 47**

Tell her to choose *any of the first 9 lines*
on that page and write down its
number.   **Line 8**

Have her choose a word on that line
from among the first 9 words and write   **Word 3**
down its number and the word.   MAGIC

Hand her the calculator and ask her to:

1. Enter the page number.   **47**

2. Multiply that number by 2. $47 \times 2 = 94$

3. Multiply that answer by 5. $94 \times 5 = 470$

4. Add 20 to that total. $470 + 20 = 490$

5. Add the line number to that
answer (*line 8*). $490 + 8 = 498$

6. Add 5 to that answer. $498 + 5 = 503$

7. Multiply that total by 10. $503 \times 10 = 5030$

8. Add the word number to that
answer (*word 3*). $5030 + 3 = 5033$

Then, tell her to hand you the calculator with the final
total.

Just subtract 250 and the page number, the line number, and the word number will magically appear!

$$
\begin{array}{cccc}
 & 5 & 0 & 3 & 3 \\
- & & 2 & 5 & 0 \\
\hline
 & 4\ 7 & 8 & 3 \\
 & \text{page} & \text{line} & \text{word}
\end{array}
$$

Turn to that page in the book, count down that many lines and over that many words, and you'll find your friend's word—MAGIC!

Exceptions

When your friend chooses a 1-digit page number, your final answer has three digits.

Example: $\underline{7}\ \underline{3}\ \underline{2}$
page line word

When your friend chooses a 3-digit page number, your final answer has five digits.

Example: $\underline{1\ 6\ 3}\ \underline{9}\ \underline{5}$
page line word

6. DICE, COINS, AND CALENDARS

DOT'S ALL, FOLKS!

X-RAY VISION

PENNIES FOR YOUR THOUGHTS

WHICH HAND?

THIS MAKES CENTS

WHAT'S THE DATE?

CALENDAR CONTEST

CALENDAR CONJURING

DOTS ALL, FOLKS!

Your friend rolls three dice when your back is turned. After performing some number magic, you are able to disclose the three top numbers on the dice!

Materials

3 dice ("Monopoly,"   A calculator
  "Yahtzee," and many other games have dice.)

Presentation

While your back is turned, have a friend:

1. Role three dice.	**Example** **3, 1, 5**
2. Multiply the top number on the first die by 2, using a calculator.	$\underline{3} \times 2 = 6$
3. Add 5 to that answer.	$6 + 5 = 11$
4. Multiply that result by 5.	$11 \times 5 = 55$
5. Add the top number on the second die to that total.	$55 + \underline{1} = 56$
6. Multiply that result by 10.	$56 \times 10 = 560$
7. Add the top number on the third die to that answer.	$560 + \underline{5} = 565$
8. Subtract 3 from that result.	$565 - 3 = 562$

Then, tell your friend to hand you the calculator with the final total. Subtract 247 and the number appears!

$$\begin{array}{r} 5\,6\,2 \\ -2\,4\,7 \\ \hline \end{array}$$

1st die $\rightarrow$ $\underline{3}\,\underline{1}\,\underline{5}$ $\leftarrow$ 3rd die
$\uparrow$
2nd die

X-RAY VISION

You throw 6 dice on the table. Before your friend can add the top numbers, you are able to add those numbers *plus* the bottom numbers that no one can see!

Materials
6 dice

Preparation
Memorize these multiples of 7:

$1 \times 7 = 7$	$6 \times 7 = 42$
$2 \times 7 = 14$	$7 \times 7 = 49$
$3 \times 7 = 21$	$8 \times 7 = 56$
$4 \times 7 = 28$	$9 \times 7 = 63$
$5 \times 7 = 35$	$10 \times 7 = 70$

Presentation

1. Tell your friend that you are going to have a contest to see who can add faster. Say that you are going to throw six dice on the table and that she should add the top numbers. Explain that you will add those numbers *plus* the hidden bottom numbers before she gets her answer.

2. Throw six dice on the table, wait two or three seconds as you pretend to add the top numbers, and then say "42!"

3. Check to see if you're correct by slowly adding the top numbers. Then carefully flip over the dice and add the bottom numbers. The total will be 42! Your friend will think that you have X-ray vision!

How to Do It

On any die, the top number plus the bottom number equals seven. So, if six dice are thrown, the total of all the tops and bottoms is:

$$6 \times 7 = 42$$
dice   total

Variations

When you repeat the trick use a different number of dice, so that you get a different total. The total will equal the number of dice $\times$ 7.

Example: 8 dice $8 \times 7 = 56$
dice   total

PENNIES FOR YOUR THOUGHTS

You secretly make a prediction before you begin. Then a friend randomly chooses five numbers and adds them together. Your prediction is unfolded and it matches his answer!

Materials

A calculator   5 pennies
Paper and pencil

Preparation

Write this grid on a piece of paper. Make it large so that you can use pennies to cover the numbers.

6	24	12	18	5
1	19	7	13	0
15	33	21	27	14
4	22	10	16	3
11	29	17	23	10

Presentation

1. Tell your friend that you are going to make a prediction. Then secretly write this on a piece of paper:

The sum of the 5 numbers that you choose will be 72

Fold your prediction several times and put it aside until later.

2. Hand your friend five pennies and ask him to place a penny on any number in the grid. Then tell him to cross off all other numbers in that same row and column.

Example: He puts a penny on 7.

6	24	12̷	18̷	5
1̷	19̷	(7)	13̷	0̷
15	33	21̷	27	14
4	22	10̷	16	3
11	29	17̷	23	10

3. Ask him to place a second penny on any other number that isn't already covered or crossed off. Then tell him to cross off all other numbers in that same row and column.

98

Example: He puts a penny on 16.

```
  6    24    1̷2̷    1̷8̷    5
  X̷    1̷0̷   ⑦     1̷3̷    X̷
 15    33    2̷1̷    2̷7̷    14
  X̷    2̷2̷   X̷     ⑯     X̷
 11    29    X̷     2̷3̷    10
```

4. Tell him to follow these same directions for the third and fourth pennies and to put the fifth penny on the last number that is not covered or crossed out.

Example: He puts the third penny on 11, the fourth penny on 33, and the fifth penny on 5.

```
  X̷    2̷4̷    1̷2̷    1̷8̷    ⑤
  X̷    1̷0̷   ⑦     1̷3̷    X̷
 1̷5̷   ㉝    2̷1̷    2̷7̷    1̷4̷
  X̷    2̷2̷   1̷0̷    ⑯     X̷
 ⑪    2̷0̷    X̷     2̷3̷    1̷0̷
```

5. Have your friend find the sum of the five numbers that he covered with the pennies and announce the total.

$$7 + 16 + 11 + 33 + 5 = 72$$

(The total will always be 72, so don't repeat this trick with the same person.)

Finally, unfold your prediction and show your friend that it matches his total!

Variations

Don't make a prediction ahead of time. After your friend

adds up the five numbers, have him concentrate on the total and pretend to read his mind.

WHICH HAND?

Your friend hides a dime in one hand and a penny in the other. After performing some hocus pocus, you are able to figure out which coin is in which hand!

Materials
A dime and a penny

Presentation
Ask your friend to put a dime in one hand and a penny in the other without letting you see. Tell her to multiply the value of the coin in her left hand by 2, 4, 6, or 8, and then multiply the value of the coin in her right hand by 3, 5, 7, or 9. Have her add these two amounts together and tell you her final total.

If her final total is *odd*, the penny is in her *right* hand.
If her final total is *even*, the penny is in her *left* hand.

Examples

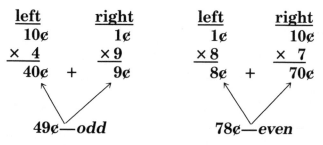

left	right	left	right
10¢	1¢	1¢	10¢
× 4	×9	×8	× 7
40¢ +	9¢	8¢ +	70¢

49¢—*odd*   78¢—*even*

So the penny is   **So the penny is**
in her *right* hand.   **in her *left* hand.**

THIS MAKES CENTS

When your back is turned, your friend arranges some pennies on the table. She removes some of the coins, and you are able to reveal the number of coins that remain!

Materials
20 to 30 pennies

Presentation
Turn your back and ask a friend to choose an odd number of pennies. Tell her to arrange them in two rows on the table so that the top row has one more coin than the bottom row.

Example: She chooses 25 coins.

1	2	3	4	5	6	7	8	9	10	11	12	13
1	2	3	4	5	6	7	8	9	10	11	12	

Next, ask her to name a number that is greater than 0 but less than the number of coins in the top row. Tell her to remove that number of coins from the top row.

Example: She says "5" (This is the *Key #*— remember it), so she removes five coins from the top row.

1	2	3	4	5	6	7	8	X	X	X	X	X
1	2	3	4	5	6	7	8	9	10	11	12	

Then have her count the number of coins remaining in the top row and remove that number of coins from the bottom row.

(There are 8 coins remaining in the top row so she removes 8 coins from the bottom row.)
Example:

1	2	3	4	5	6	7	8	X	X	X	X	X
1	2	3	4	X	X	X	X	X	X	X	X	

Finally, tell her to remove all the coins remaining in the top row. Ask her to count the number of coins remaining in the bottom row and concentrate on that number.

Example: X X X X X X X X X X X X
1 2 3 ④ X X X X X X X X

Just subtract 1 from the *Key #* and you will be able to "read her mind" and reveal the number that she is concentrating on!

Key # minus 1 = Remaining coins
in the bottom row

Example: 5 − 1 = ④

WHAT'S THE DATE?

Your friend circles three dates on a calendar, adds them together, and announces the total. Within seconds, you are able to reveal the three dates!

Materials
A calendar   A calculator

Presentation
Hand your friend the calendar and let him choose any month. Ask him to choose any three consecutive dates in a row or in a column without letting you see. Finally, tell him to add the three dates and hand you the calculator with the final total.

Examples

APRIL						
S	M	T	W	T	F	S
			1	2	3	4
5	6	7	8	9	10	11
12	13	14	15	⑯	⑰	⑱
19	20	21	22	23	24	25
26	27	28	29	30		

JUNE						
S	M	T	W	T	F	S
	1	2	3	4	5	6
⑦	8	9	10	11	12	13
⑭	15	16	17	18	19	20
㉑	22	23	24	25	26	27
28	29	30				

$$16 + 17 + 18 = 51 \qquad 7 + 14 + 21 = 42$$

Ask him if the three dates that he circled are in the same week.

If he says YES:

Divide the final total by 3 to get the middle date. Then mentally add and subtract 1 to get the other two dates.

$$51 \div 3 = 17$$
$$17 + 1 = 18$$
$$17 - 1 = 16$$

The three dates are 16, 17, & 18!

If he says NO:

Divide the final total by 3 to get the middle date. Then mentally add and subtract 7 to get the other two dates.

$$42 \div 3 = 14$$
$$14 + 7 = 21$$
$$14 - 7 = 7$$

The three dates are 7, 14, & 21!

CALENDAR CONTEST

Your friend chooses nine dates from any month on a calendar. Then you have a contest to see who can add the numbers faster. It's no contest. You win easily every time!

Materials

A calendar   Paper and pencil

A calculator

Presentation

Tell your friend that you would like to have an adding contest. Tell him that he can use a calculator and that you will use only paper and pencil. He can even choose the numbers. Who could turn down an offer like that?

Hand him the calendar and let him choose any month. Then tell him to draw a box around any group of nine numbers that form a 3 × 3 square.

Example

		FEBRUARY				
s	m	t	w	t	f	s
	1	2	3	4	5	6
7	8	9	10	11	12	13
14	15	16	17	18	19	20
21	22	23	24	25	26	27
28	29					

Whoever finds the sum of all nine numbers first is the winner. Hand him the calculator and start the contest. You will have the answer within seconds!

How to Do It

There is a trick for quickly finding the sum of all nine numbers. Just look at the smallest number, add 8, and multiply your result by 9. It works every time!

$$
\begin{array}{r}
3 \\
+\ 8 \\
\hline
11 \\
\times\ 9 \\
\hline
99
\end{array}
$$

104

CALENDAR CONJURING

You secretly make a prediction before any numbers are chosen. Then a friend chooses four dates from a calendar and adds them together. When your prediction is opened, it matches her answer!

Materials

A calculator
A calendar

Paper and pencil

Presentation

Hand your friend the calendar and let her choose any month. Then tell her to draw a box around any group of sixteen numbers that form a 4 × 4 square.

Example

NOVEMBER						
S	M	T	W	T	F	S
1	2	3	4	5	6	7
8	9	10	11	12	13	14
15	16	17	18	19	20	21
22	23	24	25	26	27	28
29	30					

As your friend is drawing the box, look at the two dates in either pair of opposite corners (3 and 27 or 6 and 24). Mentally add either pair together and multiply that sum by 2.

$$3 + 27 = 30 \text{ and } 30 \times 2 = 60$$

The final answer is your prediction. Tell your friend that you have looked into the future and have seen the sum of the four dates that she will randomly choose. Secretly write your prediction on a piece of paper, fold it several times, and put it aside until later.

Ask your friend to circle any date on the calendar. Then tell her to cross off all other dates in that same row and column.

Example: She circles 11.

NOVEMBER						
S	M	T	W	T	F	S
1	2	3	4̶	5	6	7
8	9	1̶0̶	⑪	1̶2̶	1̶3̶	14
15	16	17	1̶8̶	19	20	21
22	23	24	2̶5̶	26	27	28
29	30					

Ask her to circle any other date that isn't already circled or crossed off. Then tell her to cross off all other dates in that same row and column.

Example: She circles 26.

NOVEMBER						
S	M	T	W	T	F	S
1	2	3	4̶	5̶	6	7
8	9	1̶0̶	⑪	1̶2̶	1̶3̶	14
15	16	17	1̶8̶	1̶9̶	20	21
22	23	2̶4̶	2̶5̶	㉖	2̶7̶	28
29	30					

Tell her to follow the same directions for a third date. The fourth date will be the last number that is not circled or crossed out.

Example: She circles 17 so the fourth date is 6.

NOVEMBER						
S	M	T	W	T	F	S
1	2	3̶	4̶	5̶	⑥	7
8	9	1̶0̶	⑪	1̶2̶	1̶3̶	14
15	16	⑰	1̶8̶	1̶9̶	2̶0̶	21
22	23	2̶4̶	2̶5̶	㉖	2̶7̶	28
29	30					

Have your friend find the sum of the four dates that she circled.

$$11 + 26 + 17 + 6 = 60$$

Finally, unfold the paper and show that your prediction matches her final answer!

106

7. EXTRA FOR EXPERTS

YOUNG GENIUS

Your friends will think that you are ready for college when you add five large numbers in your head in just a few seconds!

Materials

Paper and pencil   A calculator

Preparation

Write this chart on a piece of paper.

A	B	C	D	E
366	345	186	872	756
69	840	582	971	558
168	246	87	575	657
762	147	285	377	954
960	543	483	179	855
564	48	780	674	459

Presentation

While your back is turned, have a friend choose *one number* from each of the five columns and write them on a piece of paper. Tell her to add the five numbers using a calculator and write the answer underneath.

Example

762
246
483
674
+ 756
2,921

Finally, ask her to read off slowly the five numbers in any order so that you can add them in your head. You will have the answer in seconds!

How to Do It

As your friend reads the five numbers, just mentally add the *five last digits*.

$$2 + 6 + 3 + 4 + 6 = \underline{21}$$

Mentally subtract this sum from 50.

$$50 - 21 = \underline{29}$$

Put the second number in front of the first number to get the sum of all five numbers!

$$\underline{2, 9\ 21}!$$

PHOTOGRAPHIC MEMORY

Your friends are really impressed when you show them that you have memorized fifty different 6-digit and 7-digit numbers!

Materials

50 index cards   Paper and pencil

Preparation

Copy these numbers onto index cards—one to each card. The card number appears in italics.

1	5,055,055	*11*	5,167,303	*21*	5,279,651
2	6,066,280	*12*	6,178,538	*22*	6,280,886
3	7,077,415	*13*	7,189,763	*23*	7,291,011
4	8,088,640	*14*	8,190,998	*24*	8,202,246
5	9,099,875	*15*	9,101,123	*25*	9,213,471
6	112,358	*16*	224,606	*26*	336,954
7	1,123,583	*17*	1,235,831	*27*	1,347,189
8	2,134,718	*18*	2,246,066	*28*	2,358,314
9	3,145,943	*19*	3,257,291	*29*	3,369,549
10	4,156,178	*20*	4,268,426	*30*	4,370,774

31	5,381,909	*41*	5,493,257
32	6,392,134	*42*	6,404,482
33	7,303,369	*43*	7,415,617
34	8,314,594	*44*	8,426,842
35	9,325,729	*45*	9,437,077
36	448,202	*46*	550,550
37	1,459,437	*47*	1,561,785
38	2,460,662	*48*	2,572,910
39	3,471,897	*49*	3,583,145
40	4,482,022	*50*	4,594,370

Example

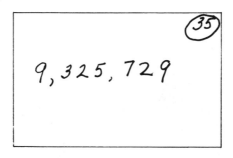

Presentation

Shuffle the deck of index cards so that they are not in order, and then hand them to your friend. Tell her that there is a different number written on each card and that you have memorized all fifty numbers. Ask her to choose any card. When she tells you the card number, you are able to tell her which 6-digit or 7-digit number is on that card!

How to Do It

1. When your friend tells you the card number, mentally add 4 and then reverse your answer. The result is the first two digits.

Example: Card #35
35 + 4 = 39 and 39 reversed is 93.

The first two digits are 93.

2. To get the next digit, mentally add the first two digits together. If this sum is less than 10, write it down. If it is 10 or greater, only write down the number that is in the ones place.

$$9 + 3 = 1\underline{2} \qquad\qquad 93\underline{2}$$

3. Continue adding the last two digits to get the next one until you have written down all seven digits.

$$3 + 2 = \underline{5} \qquad 932\underline{5}$$
$$2 + 5 = \underline{7} \qquad 9325\underline{7}$$
$$5 + 7 = 1\underline{2} \qquad 93257\underline{2}$$
$$7 + 2 = \underline{9} \qquad 932572\underline{9}$$

Answer: 9,325,729

Exceptions

If your friend picks a card number that ends in 6, the number on that card has only six digits.

Example: Card #36
36 + 4 = 40 and 40 reversed is 04
The number is 0,448,202

(Don't say "Zero")——↑

If your friend picks a card number from 1 to 5, mentally put a zero in the tens place before reversing your answer.

Example: Card #3
3 + 4 = 7 and 07 reversed is 70
The number is 7,077,415

A Variation
You can work the trick backwards. Tell your friend to give you the 6-digit or 7-digit number, and then you tell her the card number! When she tells you the number, reverse the first two digits and then subtract 4 to get the card number.

Example: The number is 1,235,831
12 reversed is 21 and 21 − 4 = 17
The card number is 17.

An Exception to This Variation
If your friend gives you a 6-digit number, mentally put the zero back in front, and then work the trick backwards.

Example: The number is 336,954
(0,336,954)

03 reversed is 30 and 30 − 4 = 26
The card number is 26.

BRAIN POWER

Your friends will think that you are an amazing number magician when you find the sum of ten numbers in just a few seconds!

Materials

A calculator   Paper and pencil

Preparation

Write the numbers 1–10 on a piece of paper, one under the other.

Presentation

1. Tell your friend to write any 1-digit number on the first line and a different 1-digit number on the second line.

Example 5 and 9

1. 5

2. Ask him to add these two numbers together and write their sum on the third line.

2. 9

$$5 + 9 = 14$$

3. 14

3. Have him add line 2 and line 3 and write that sum on the fourth line.

4. 23

$$9 + 14 = 23$$

5. 37

4. Tell him to continue adding in this manner until there is a list of ten numbers. Make sure that he is adding correctly. Each number in the list (except the first two) must be the sum of the two numbers above it.

6. 60

7. 97

8. 157

9. 254

10. 411

When your friend writes down the last number, quickly

114

look at his list and pretend that you are adding all ten numbers in your head. Secretly write your answer on a piece of paper, fold it several times, and put it aside. Ask your friend to slowly add all ten numbers, using a calculator.

(Example: 1,067)

He will be amazed when you unfold the paper and your answer matches his final total!

How to Do It

When ten numbers are added in this manner,
The Final Total = the seventh number × 11!
So when you look at your friend's list, just look at the seventh number. Multiply that number by 11 on your piece of paper to get the final total.

Here is a quick way to multiply by 11:
Multiply the seventh number by 10. (97 × 10) 970
Add the seventh number to that answer. +   97
  1,067

Cross off your work so that your friend does not discover your secret. Make it look as if you have underlined your answer.

A Variation

Start with two 2-digit numbers and your friends will really be amazed!

115

MYSTERY POWDER

You and your friend write down five 4-digit numbers and add them using a calculator. When your secret mystery powder is rubbed over a piece of plastic, the correct answer magically appears!

Materials

A calculator
Paper and pencil
Glue stick
Ground cinnamon

Any piece of white plastic, such as the white lid from a plastic container

Preparation

Put a small amount of cinnamon or any dark spice into a small container. This is the mystery powder.

Write a number in the 20,000's on a piece of white plastic with a glue stick.

Example: 23,156

This is the Final Total. The number should be invisible yet remain sticky.

116

Figure out your *Key #*. First add 2 to the Final Total, and then cross off the first digit of your answer.

$$\begin{array}{r} 23{,}156 \\ +2 \\ \hline 23{,}158 \\ \textit{Key \#} \end{array}$$

Presentation

1. Ask a friend to write a 4-digit number on a piece of paper. The digits must be different and not form a pattern.

Example
8,351

2. You write the *Key #*. ⟶ **3,158**

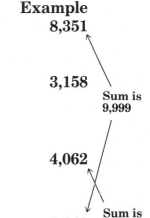

Sum is 9,999

3. Tell your friend to write a different 4-digit number below your number.

4,062

4. You write a 4-digit number so that the sum of the first and fourth numbers = 9,999.

1,648 Sum is 9,999

5. You write a 4-digit number so that the sum of the third and fifth numbers = 9,999.

5,937

Give your friend the piece of paper and ask him to add the five numbers using a calculator.

(23,156)

Sprinkle your mystery powder over the piece of white plastic, and then perform some hocus pocus as you rub it around. Blow off the excess powder and—like magic—the Final Total mysteriously appears!

An Exception

Your friend writes a 9 for the first digit of the first number or the third number.

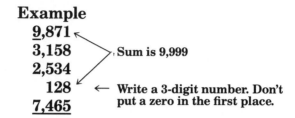

Example
<u>9</u>,871
3,158 } Sum is 9,999
2,534
128 ← Write a 3-digit number. Don't
<u>7,465</u> put a zero in the first place.

HAS ANYONE SEEN A GHOST?

This is a trick that you can do for a group of your friends or relatives. A prediction is put inside a shoe box and three random numbers are added using a calculator. When the shoe box is opened, your incorrect prediction has been mysteriously replaced by the correct answer!

Materials

A calculator
Shoe box
Marker
An index card
Pencil

A small spiral notebook
that looks the same
no matter which side
is up

Preparation

1. Write any 4-digit number on an index card with a marker, then cross it off. This is your prediction. Write a different 4-digit number (between 1000 and 2000) below the first number. Make it look like this number was written by a ghost. Put the card face down on the table.

2. Open the notebook to the middle and write down three 3-digit numbers. Make it look as if each 3-digit number was written by a different person. The sum of these numbers should equal the ghostly number on the piece of paper. Turn the notebook over and put it on the table with the blank side up.

```
526
847
470
```

Performance

Give the calculator to a friend who is in the back of the room and tell him that you will need his help later.

Show your friends that there is nothing inside the shoe box, and then put your prediction and the marker inside. Put the top on the shoe box and give it to your friend to hold.

Ask another friend to come up to the table and write a 3-digit number on the blank page in the notebook. Repeat this with two other friends. Don't let anyone turn over the notebook.

When the third number is written down, pick up the notebook and take it to your friend with the calculator.

As you are walking over to your friend, *secretly turn over the notebook*. Show him the top page (*your* three numbers) and ask him to add the three numbers using the calculator. Close the notebook so that no one sees the other side. Tell your friend to announce the answer.

When your friend says the answer, look disappointed and admit that your prediction in the shoe box is incorrect. Make up a story about a ghost who is a friend of yours and explain that he will assist you with the trick. Ask your invisible friend to enter the shoe box, pick up the marker, cross off your prediction, and write the correct answer underneath. Repeat the answer one more time and then ask your friend to remove the piece of paper from the shoe box. To everyone's surprise, your ghostly assistant has saved the day by writing the correct answer below your prediction!

THE HUMAN COMPUTER

You can astound your friends by adding five 6-digit numbers in just a few seconds!

Materials

A calculator   Paper and pencil

Presentation

1. Ask a friend to write a 6-digit number on a piece of paper. The digits must be different and not form a pattern.

2. Tell her to write a second 6-digit number below her first number.

3. Ask her to write one more number. This third number is your *Key #*. ———→

4. You write a 6-digit number so that the sum of the first and the fourth numbers = 999,999.

5. You write a 6-digit number so that the sum of the second and fifth numbers = 999,999.

Example

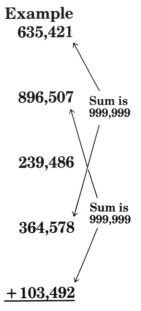

635,421

896,507   Sum is
           999,999

239,486

                Sum is
364,578   999,999

+ 103,492

Give your friend the piece of paper and ask her to add the five numbers using a calculator without letting you see the Final Total—

(2,239,484).

When she hands you the paper, pretend that you are adding the five numbers in your head and quickly write down the Final Total!

How to Do It

When your friend hands you the paper, just look at the *Key #*, because the Final Total = 2,————

(*Key #* minus 2).

121

Example:
Key # is 239,486
(Key # minus 2) = 239,484

The Final Total = 2,239,484

An Exception

Your friend writes a 9 for the first digit of the first number or the second number.

Example

$\underline{9}56,231$ ⤸
$623,178$ **Sum is 999,999**
$279,651$ ⤹
$\ \ 43,768$ ← **Write a 5-digit number. Don't**
$\underline{376,821}$ **put a zero in the first place.**

Variations

Seven 6-digit numbers:
    The Final Total = 3,_____
                     (Key # minus 3)

Nine 6-digit numbers:
    The Final Total = 4,_____
                     (Key # minus 4)

PSYCHIC PREDICTION

You are able to predict the sum of five 5-digit numbers before the trick begins! Also, when the digits of this sum are translated into letters, they spell your friend's name!

Materials
Paper and pencil   A calculator

Preparation
Write this chart on a piece of paper.

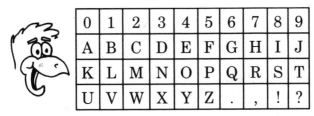

0	1	2	3	4	5	6	7	8	9
A	B	C	D	E	F	G	H	I	J
K	L	M	N	O	P	Q	R	S	T
U	V	W	X	Y	Z	.	,	!	?

Pick a friend who has three to six letters for a first or last name. (See *Variations* for more ideas.) The first letter must be a letter in the 2-column—C, M, or W.

Example: Cosby

Use the chart to translate your friend's name into a 6-digit number. This number is the Predicted Sum.

Cosby!
248,148

Figure out your *Key #*. Just add 2 to the Predicted Sum, and then cross off the first digit of your answer.

$$248{,}148$$
$$+\qquad 2$$

Presentation $\quad$ ⟍248,150

Announce that you will write down the answer to a math problem before any numbers are given. Write the Predicted Sum on another piece of paper, fold it several times, and put it aside until later.

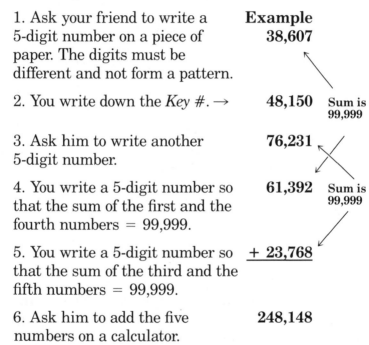

1. Ask your friend to write a 5-digit number on a piece of paper. The digits must be different and not form a pattern.

Example
38,607

2. You write down the *Key #*. →

48,150 Sum is 99,999

3. Ask him to write another 5-digit number.

76,231

4. You write a 5-digit number so that the sum of the first and the fourth numbers = 99,999.

61,392 Sum is 99,999

5. You write a 5-digit number so that the sum of the third and the fifth numbers = 99,999.

+ 23,768

6. Ask him to add the five numbers on a calculator.

248,148

Finally, unfold your prediction and show your friend that it matches his answer! Then use the chart to translate his answer into letters and his name will magically appear!

248,148
COSBY!

Variations for Choosing a Name

MR.C.!   MS.G.!   MRBLUM   MSROTH   MRS.J.

Other Variations

You could make words appear.

Example: MONDAY, MATH!!, MAGIC!, COLD!!, WEIGHT, etc.

Use your imagination! You could also rearrange the chart so that different letters appear in the 2-column. Then you could make many more names or words appear!

An Exception

Your friend writes a 9 for the first digit of the first number or the third number.

Example

$\underline{9}2,761$

48,150   **Sum is 99,999**

49,135

7,238 ← **Write a 4-digit number. Don't**

+ 50,864   **put a zero in the first place.**

248,148

COSBY!

INDEX

ABOUT THE AUTHOR

Raymond Blum has been a middle-level math teacher for over 20 years. On weekends and in the summer, he entertains professionally with his daughter, Katie. Their stage show is called, "Raynbow and The Amazing Kaytee's Juggling & Magic Show." He has been a speaker at state and national math conferences where he shares his "Razzle Dazzle Number Magic" with other classroom teachers. Ray is currently teaching seventh grade at Schenk Middle School in Madison, Wisconsin.